Thinking of
Dinner at Lunch

Thinking of Dinner at Lunch

COLE FELDMAN

Thinking of Dinner at Lunch
Copyright © 2023 by Cole Feldman

This book is creative writing in the forms of poetry and prose. It is intended to be a work of art for entertainment purposes only. Its contents do not necessarily convey an accurate account of real events and should not be taken as a source of advice. The author and publisher do not assume and hereby disclaim any liability to any party for any loss or damage allegedly caused as a consequence (direct or indirect) of the contents of this book.

www.colefeldman.net

ISBN: 0-9963608-6-7
ISBN-13: 978-0-9963608-6-9

Cover designer: Sabina Kencana

CONTENTS

~

I. GROCERY STORES STILL AMAZE ME

II. THE ONLY HONEST REVOLUTION

III. KANSAS

IV. ESCAPISM

V. A POET WITHOUT A MUSE

VI. THE OTHER GUYS

VII. EXISTENTIAL ANXIETY

VIII. EVENING-ONSET THANATOPHOBIA

IX. EGO DEATH

GROCERY STORES STILL AMAZE ME

WHAT'S LEFT

When sex
Isn't secret anymore

When the drugs are all done
And the highs are familiar

When you get what you wanted
And it's still not enough

When you lose faith in religion
And give up on philosophy

When the movie plots are predictable
And the songs sound the same

When your dad's beard grows on your own chin
And you've seen all the colors of the leaves

When the airlines take you wherever you want to go
And each new place looks like the last

When a younger man calls you mister
And you realize the adults didn't know any better

When the old games are no longer fun
And the new games are the old games in disguise

When the end seems closer than the beginning
And the sky seems closer to the ground

When afternoon becomes evening
And evening becomes night

I sleep in the fetal position
And dream of being born again

ANOTHER COG COMING OF AGE

I grew up in the grocery store
Begging my mom for sugar cereal

Instead of kneeling in the field
Praying for rain

Learned to write in cursive
Instead of hunting horseback

Went to college on government loans
Instead of walking to the water

Got my first job in a big city
Instead of following the herd

Now I collect paychecks
And buy my own groceries

Instead of rising with the sun
And moving with the wind

MODERN BEAUTY

In a sunset, I see beauty that might have meant more, if I had been born outdoors.

If I had needed wood for a fire to keep warm.

If rainfall had meant the buffalo would come to the water in three moons.

But now I see beauty in bathtubs and grocery stores with stocked shelves.

On the dinner table and between the drapes.

In the corner of a room where two walls meet the floor.

Along the line where building tops border the bleeding sky.

I GUESS I'LL HAVE THE OCTOPUS

The menu
Has more pages
Than a novel

Groceries
Get delivered
To your door

Robots
Write poetry

Cars
Drive themselves

But the smokestacks
Still fume

Cargo ships
Crowd the bay

Young men
Labor for love

Old women
Try to buy beauty

Until the ozone
Evaporates

And all the ice caps
Have melted

LEFTOVER CHILI

The wind blowing the leaves
And the sirens outside
Are too obvious

I can hear her sighs
Through the open door
Across the hall

The dog upstairs
Runs back and forth
But doesn't bark

The wind sounds like
A rainstick
Full of waves

The kitchen light
Makes a buzzing noise
That I've gotten used to

The waves wash over
The sirens come for
The dog runs toward

Someone
Somewhere else

THINKING OF DINNER AT LUNCH

Even
When I get
What I wanted

It's brief
Before another want
Assails me

I've tried
To not want

But I fail
Before I start

Because wanting
To not want
Is still wanting

I FORGET TO BE GRATEFUL

A woman holds hands with a blind man, leading him
into the coffee shop.

I imagine never being able to see my lover again.

How much I have to lose.

So many gifts I've been given.

And all I do most of the time is want more.

When I should really just sit down and look at
everything and smile.

THE ONLY HONEST REVOLUTION

ALL GOOD ON THE DANCE FLOOR

The techno kids in
The club can't even
Keep step with the beat they're
So drugged out that
Any music moves them any
Noise no matter how
Dissonant no
Matter how loud as
Long as the lights are
Strobing and the crowd is
Still around the
Techno kids swing their arms and
Stomp their feet and
Shake their hands and
Smile at the ceiling with
Their eyes closed because
On the drugs it's
All good even
When it seems to
Be the music it's
Really just pupils
Dilating arteries
Opening heart
Beating there's
Blood on the dance floor but
It's all in bodies so
It's all good

IT ALL INTERSECTS

At that ephemeral place of knowing where only drug
trippers, mystics, and a few physicists occasionally visit

Where LSD, Jesus Christ, and quantum theory convene

The bass beats coming from the speakers at night teach
me the same lesson as the poetry handbook I read at
the laundromat in the morning

The music stops, but I keep dancing

Because even when the businessman walks to work, his
steps land on the sidewalk in a rhythm

As a thousand office workers in skyscrapers type out a
symphony on their keyboards

As I try to figure out the difference between stressed
and unstressed syllables, even though I'm tone deaf

On drugs it's easy to see it's all the same

FOREST FESTIVAL

"If you're an artist and you perform on this stage, you must think, I've made it."

What's after you make it?

The kids in front of us draw and smoke cigarettes.

She has a pen behind her ear, bobs her head, cool like.

"Shit's right."

Dialogue from the TV show last night.

"We should eat the rest of the mushrooms."

Okay.

Robots can't write this.

Can't feel the sun coming through the clouds.

Hear the subtleties in the singer's voice that sound like she knows.

Like the experience she had growing up in Baltimore and going to church.

One of those churches where people get filled with the spirit and fall down.

That stuck with her.

The crowd obeys the music like the waves obey the moon.

Every drop in the ocean is individual yet together.

I look at people's faces and feel that I am them.

I used to feel the need to write whenever I experienced altered states.

I felt like I had to take field notes to bring back to my sober life.

My spiritual progress can be measured by the decrease in my will to write.

I used to pick flowers to bring back to my lover.

But she's here with me now.

We lie back on the blanket and look up at the leaves shaking in the breeze, sunlight shimmering in between.

It feels right right now.

A million flowers bloom in my mind, but I resist the urge to write them.

My editor says the mantras are too cliché anyway.

It is what it is.

And it's right right now.

HALCYON

How does the light shine
In mid-air
Like there's something there
To catch it
Hold it
Have it happen to be
The blue, green
Yellow I can see
Her face
For a few seconds
As the lights strobe
Shadows shoot across
She says
She can hear the lights
Then darkness
That has no beauty
No sense
Just nothing
For my eyes at least
My ears still thud
Then the strobes again
And her face
And beauty

VESUVIO

What a life
Wood
Under my banging fist
Solid
Something real
My martini
Is mostly gin
Music plays
People talk
The bartenders
Take shots together
Glasses clink
In the dishwasher
The ceiling
Has been painted over
Who knows
How many times
Everyone shouts
At each other
Over the music
And it doesn't matter
If we understand
It was never the words
It was always
The subtle sound
The brush of skin
The accidental glance

The all-knowing
Ever present
As I bang my fist
On the wooden railing
It's here
And I can feel it
Pushing back
Behind the bar
On crowded shelves
Glass bottles glow
Drinks are made
Tabs are paid
Patrons have come
Drunk, laughed
And left
Like we all leave
Eventually
You can't come
And not go
Stay, leave
It's all the same
Somewhere
Between hello
And goodbye
The lemon twist
At the bottom of my glass
The olive
At the bottom of hers
The businessman

Talking loudly
About his business
Wishing someone
Would listen
The young kids
Continue drinking
The lampshade
Sings a song
Of swaying
That sounds like
A lullaby
I close my eyes
And slip away

THE FACTORY

The only light
Comes from the bulbs
Behind the bottles
On the shelves
Shaking
In sync
With the bass
Beating
In my chest
An excess
Of alcohol
Isn't enough
Anymore
To escape my thoughts
Of the inevitable
I dance
Harder
Bend my knees
Deeper
Throw my hands
Higher
Shake my head
Stomp
Striving
In vain
To dissociate
To slip off

Into the black void
Behind my eyelids
But I can't
Quite
Get there
Get past
The threshold
That separates
Divine dance
From death despair
I drink
More
Dance
More
Until I finally
Feel that I am
Myself
Less
More together
With the rest
More comfortable
To close my eyes
And stop seeing
As separate
The girl glancing
The guy posturing
I focus
On feeling
The floor

Under our feet
The glass
Against my fingertips
As appearances
Undress
And death
Seems less
Like the end

KANSAS

WHAT I HEAR WHILE LYING IN THE DARK AT 6:10 A.M.

The static, salt-and-pepper channel on TV, turned down to the lowest volume. Or a million bugs in the trees at night. Not big, loud cicadas. More like little flies, whispering softly. And so many of them. *Sssssss.*

The sound is continuous. There is no inbreath, no interruption. Just a constant, slightly high-pitched exhale. Because of the continuity, I assume the onomatopoeia for silence should have only one letter.

I say the alphabet in my head, trying out different letters, mouthing each sound aloud to check if it matches the silence, as a singer tries to match the note being played.

Ttttttt. Yes, maybe 't' is closer. Actually, more like this: *teeeeeee.* But there can only be one letter. So maybe just 'e' then. *Eeeeeeee.* It's a "long" 'e,' as in the word 'be.' *Eeeeeeee.* Yes, that is my best guess, for now.

IT WAS 80 AND SUNNY IN SHAWNEE TODAY

My mom always wondered how it got so dirty.

The smell of asphalt on a hot day reminds me of recess.

We played kickball in the parking lot.

Dirt from the ball and sweat filled the wrinkles in my hands with lines of mud.

I wiped them on my white uniform shirt.

PORNO MAG

There were about two hundred kids out at recess. On the jungle gym. In the parking lot playing kickball. Running through the trees, pretending to be horses.

All of a sudden, there was a mad rush to the soccer field. I fought my way through the crowd—slipping past arms, crawling between legs.

Once I found the center, I got one glimpse of what was causing the commotion, before a teacher reached in and snatched it away.

A picture in a magazine of a naked woman in a bathtub.

In an instant, I learned more about the world—why wars are fought, why poetry is written, why humans keep on living and dying—than I had from all my schooling.

A DOG BARKED

In the backyard
Behind the fence

As I walked by
On the sidewalk

I looked at the dog
But there was nothing to say

The dog kept barking
And I kept walking

IN THE PARK

I was lying on my back in the grass.

The ball rolled toward me.

A young boy came running over with his hands held open.

I picked it up and threw it back to him.

THUNDERSTORM

A lightning strike is as many miles away as the number of seconds that pass between when you see the lightning and when you hear the thunder.

We kept the back door open.

Rain pattered on the fallen leaves in the yard.

Through the window, a lightning flash illuminated the cars in the driveway, the neighbor's fence, the pond in the distance.

I counted the seconds … one, two, three …

Four seconds.

Then thunder rumbled to the northwest.

Four miles away, someone didn't even get to one.

A MORNING ON THE CUSP OF WINTER

The clouds overhead form an expansive layer of blueish-gray with splotches of white where the sun almost breaks through.

Brown leaves lie in piles in the yard. The few remaining on the trees rustle as the wind blows.

One bird chirps monotonously. Other birds sing sporadically.

The squirrels chase each other along branches, nimbly hopping between trees, blending in against the bark.

Now that the leaves have dropped like a curtain, you can see beyond the tree line.

Geese graze in the grass by the pond.

Cars drive along the highway.

An unseen plane flies audibly above the cloud layer.

A STORY THAT GRANDPA TOLD AFTER DINNER TONIGHT

When he was a kid, Grandpa, his siblings, and their neighborhood friends slept in the backyard some nights. They had army tents that were long and triangular with two walls and no floor.

After their parents went to bed, they crawled out of their tents and snuck over to the golf course. They went to the fourth hole because that was the hole with the water hazard.

They rolled up their pant legs and stepped around in the shallow parts of the pond, picking up golf balls with their toes.

GRANDPA TALKING ABOUT HIS SISTER

You should read it, really. I would give you my copy,
but I already gave it to my sister. She ain't gonna read it
though.

She was a flower child.

She brought this guy to Thanksgiving one year. He was
wearing a military jacket down to his ankles and a beard
down to his belt. He wouldn't eat the turkey. Said he
was a vegetarian. But he was putting gravy on his
mashed potatoes. So I told him, don't eat any of that
gravy either.

She dated another guy who drove an eighteen-wheeler.
He would park it outside the house. One day, I think he
even drove the kids to school in that thing.

She was so far to the left she was going to fall off the
earth.

ESCAPISM

THE SONG OF FOUR FRIENDS PLAYING CARDS

I lay in the loft and tried to sleep but gave up on avoiding listening to my friends downstairs playing euchre and talking about the cities they each wanted to move to and opened my eyes and stared at the cedar ceiling and listened to learn what I could from the words and maybe end up falling asleep to them like a bedtime story and even if not oh well this too shall pass and this is a good opportunity to practice letting go of my desires like wanting to fall asleep and instead meditating on the present listening to the words not only as vehicles of meaning driving from their mouths to my ears but also as just sounds like what I read in a spiritual book about how when you look and see a dog it's already something before you say in your mind oh that's a dog it's the color and the shape as if you were seeing a dog for the first time not knowing you could walk up and feel its fur so I lay and listened and tried to just hear the noise and wonder what is sound what are these noises laughs exclamations interruptions oohs and aahs glasses being set down on the table cards being shuffled all together the art of the opposite of a silent movie a pictureless film with only one long song for its soundtrack the song of four friends playing cards in the living room at night.

HOLY MAN ON THE PLANE TO SALT LAKE CITY

While I was waiting in the aisle, I looked down the row
to my right and saw him in the middle seat.

Even without the obvious signs of religiosity—

white woven cap on his shaved head,
unpretentious reading glasses sliding down his nose,
long scraggly beard,
white robes hemmed with ornate gold lace

—I would have still recognized him as a holy man
because of the way he had his

arms crossed,
hands tucked under his armpits,
eyes closed,
head nodding slightly forward.

He wasn't sleeping.

While everyone else watched the seatback screens and
scrolled on their phones,

he sat in silence and prayed for us all.

A TRANSIENT WALKS BY A RESTAURANT IN SAN FRANCISCO

He shuffles his feet on the sidewalk, pants sagging, folded newspaper hanging out of his back pocket.

A jazz band stands by, holding their instruments idly between songs. People eat and talk at tables outside the restaurant. Cutlery clinks on porcelain plates.

He starts to shout, something indiscernible, motioning erratically. People stop eating and stare.

Nobody does or says anything. They hold forks and knives in frozen hands.

He stops shouting and just stands there. For a moment, there is silence, other than distant sirens.

Then he turns and staggers on down the sidewalk.

Cutlery continues clinking. The band picks up their instruments and carries on with the next song.

SAD ACCORDION PLAYER

On the sidewalk in Sintra
He held his accordion
Like it was his last hope
Leaning
With his ear
Near enough to the keys
To hear his fingers pressing
Hunched over
Hugging the instrument
Like a lover
About to leave him
Looking over his knees
At only a few coins
In the open case
At his feet

DRINKING SANGRIA AS THE SUN SETS IN PORTO

There is a constant flow of people walking out of the door to the bar with full glasses in their hands.

Most tables on the patio have two or three talking eagerly to each other.

The hum of conversation is like a pressed piano key, but any one exchange is incomprehensible, in a language I don't understand.

Some stand from their tables and disappear down cobblestone sidewalks.

Seagulls fly overhead as the ladies put out their cigarettes in the ashtray.

It's almost impossible to imagine this will ever end, that the energy will dissipate and eventually be totally gone.

But surely, as at the end of all nights, the umbrellas will be drawn down, the chairs will be folded, the tables will be carried inside, and the patio will be empty.

All through the dark night. And all through the day. Until the sun is almost setting again.

And then the tables will be brought back out and the chairs will be unfolded. The umbrellas will be extended and the first patrons will arrive to order their drinks.

And then more will come and again everyone will be drinking and talking.

DESSERT AT DESPENSA

The gelato dripped slowly
Down the side of the cake

While we waited for the waiter
To bring an extra plate

THE OLD MAN'S ADVICE

The irony of it all is that the advice the old Parisian man gave you at the café by the park as you sipped rosé and ate macarons is the same advice you'll be giving to another young man a generation from now.

But this time you'll pay the bill.

And the young man won't listen.

Just like you didn't listen.

Because the advice never makes sense until you've lived it, until you've become the old man.

And then you want to give the advice to a younger man.

And so it goes, generation to generation.

We learn how to live just in time to die.

A POET WITHOUT A MUSE

SILENT MUSE

In the dark my
Muse lies honestly
About what a body can say to
Searching lips seeking for
Only one truth to whisper
Only one song to sing
Only if she'd open her mouth
The poems would pour
And pour
And she knows this
But still stays silent in the dark
Singing to herself
Sorry that the world of man
Will always want more

WHEN SHE'S GONE

Her coat
Hangs over the back

Of the empty chair
I stare

Look down at my drink
And listen

To the other tables talking
To the forks fencing knives
To the yawning sound

Of a great void
Within me
When she's gone

ABSTINENCE

My desire for her wells without release. I am unequipped to sink as deeply into the ocean of her as my heart alone would, if it were not encased in this clumsy corporal container. I pull her body close to mine, constrict her in my embrace until she says I must be gentle. But still, she comes not near enough.

The water to which my lustful flesh would lead my horse heart is an obvious innuendo. A banality, it has become, as I have habitually drunk from that fount. Over and over, I have splashed like a child in the shallows and held my breath to swim deep into the depths, but I never reach the bottom and always return to the surface, gasping for air, exclaiming, "There is no end to this wonder!"

Swimming starts to seem like walking to one who has spent so long in the water. If the merman were to be fished out and made to walk, where would his desire to swim satiate itself? Bathing in public water fountains, perusing aquatic aisles at pet stores.

It is agony, yes, but sweet agony. Like hunger before a meal. The first bite is the best. The second and third are increasingly unconvincing impostors of the true taste in the first. Even before the first bite, what taste is there already in hunger? Standing in the kitchen, smell is weak foreplay for the sense of the tongue. Far away from even hope of food, stranded in the desert, memories of taste would remain.

But here I am, in an oasis of her—sleeping in the same bed, holding her. All but the deep drink. Like Tantalus, except the fruit places itself in my palm and the water rises to my lips, and it is only my own obstinate attempts to channel my natural inclinations elsewhere that keep me from biting into the forbidden and drinking the holy.

But not all in vain. I have felt the force of a dammed river pumping in my veins, and thus have understood the story about the old sage who, when asked about love, led his young student on a journey in the rain.

First, to the mountain peak above the clouds. Then, down into the valley, as the rain flooded into the river. And finally, to the coastal cliffs, where the river emptied into the ocean.

In order to test the young student's comprehension, the old sage asked him, "Where will we go next?"

The student looked out at the sea, then back at the sage, and said, "Back up the mountain, into the clouds."

The old sage smiled, closed his eyes, and nodded.

LITTLE LEAVINGS

I leave her a little
Each time I walk away

Even from the kitchen
To the dining room

I want to hurry back
And hold her again

I THOUGHT I HEARD HER CRYING

I couldn't tell if it was just the music, or if she really was up there whimpering. I got up and walked over to the steep, ladder-like steps of the water-tower-turned-cabin, grabbed the railing, and climbed up.

There she was: caramel skin in contrast with the white sheets, curly hair slightly frizzy (as it gets when she's been rolling around in bed). I asked how she was doing, if she was okay (I forget exactly what I said). We skated, as we tend to, like those water bugs, along the surface, before descending.

Then she told me that she *had* been crying. I said, oh, I'm sorry, well, that is why I came up here, to check on you. She said, oh, did you hear me? You couldn't have. It was only a tear. I wasn't sobbing. I told her I thought I had heard crying, but maybe it was just the music. We marveled. I must have *felt* her crying, somehow.

She was crying because she thought of her mom as she read a few pages of a book she found on the steps. It was written by a Vietnamese author (my girlfriend's mother is Vietnamese). The pages were about how the author was thankful for his mother and for memories of when she would take him to the mall.

She said, I realized I want to cry more. I want to have things in my life that make me cry. Not just shallow melodrama. You know? Like (and she proceeded to describe what she meant and how she felt in words that were perfect, but all I can remember is …) things that make you feel like you're on the brink of being alive.

The moment was sublime, terribly so. I, knowing our relationship was ending, one tear already on my cheek and more welling. Her, beautiful in her body, but then also the depths and intricacies of her emotions, as well as her lexical prowess to communicate them. The trees through the window behind her, bending in the wind, a glint on the glass making their green look red.

Gah! What is a man to do? Other than audibly call for his deity, cry more than he already has, shield his eyes, only to pry them back open, unveiling the portal to his soul, inviting in the moment that is more than can be captured by any artist, no matter how skilled.

In that moment, the potency of a lifetime was distilled down into one drink, one swallow. As soon as it touched my lips, I sputtered and spat.

If it were watered down and spread out so that I could have had time to process, make rational, cram into my own understanding—then perhaps I could have taken it. As it was—me, her, and the trees through the window behind her—I had to run.

It took some willpower and a great deal more conditioned concern for my bodily well-being not to suddenly fling myself down the steep steps as fast and as recklessly as my heart and soul were fleeing. But no matter the manner in which I did, I ran, nonetheless.

I ran as I always do. I ran like a thief into a field clutching above my head the bouquet of flowers she had given me, petals flying off them as I went.

See, I've never been able to stay put there and just listen to her. As soon as she starts being beautiful (which is immediately and always), I run away with my derivatives, hand-me-downs of her to render into my art, so that others will pay me, praise me, or whatever will validate the male equivalent of female beauty.

I do this, even as I am somewhat aware that I am running in a wide circle, the path of which is littered with obstacles, deceits, let-downs, repetitive exhaustion, self-loathing, and various other trials that must be faced by a man working his way up through the world to be worthy of a woman at the top.

All of this, I persist in putting myself through, even as the woman of my dreams lies here in bed, asking me,

why won't you listen? Why won't you come to bed?
Why won't you stay?

HEROINE WITHDRAWALS

So this is what it's like
To have everything
And lose it all

To hold an angel in your arms
And let her fly away

To stay in bed for days
Because all you've ever wanted
Is in the sheets with you
And then try to sleep alone

I try convincing myself
It would have been better
If I'd never felt her love

But of course not
Because as low as the low is now
The high was even higher

And I'd walk on glass for miles
Burn for years
And take even more pain
Than the space of my body can contain
For one more night with her

BEAUTY IS BECOME HER

When the faceless women in my dreams take off their clothes, they have her breasts, her bronze skin, her hip bones that jut out.

I remember—before I first loved her—my friend told me that he thought she was beautiful.

When I saw her next, I decided that I agreed with him.

I agreed because she had certain qualities in common with my idea of beauty at the time.

Now, when I'm in the checkout aisle at the grocery store and I look over the shelves of candy and see a woman with dark curly hair, freckled cheeks, and perfectly straight white teeth, she is beautiful because of her likeness to Her.

Only, I have not met such a woman.

Nor do I think I ever will, as she told me before I left.

LOVE POEM

buh-BUM
buh-BUM
buh-BUM

Beating on
In eternal
Iambic

THE OTHER GUYS

WHEN GOD BECAME MAN

A beautiful man stood on the sidewalk
With his hands in his pockets
Looking like a god

Then he scrunched his nose
Threw his head back
And sneezed

And I thought, ah
He is a man
So I blessed him

HOW HE WALKED

He didn't have his shoulders thrown back or his chest puffed out. Not like a businessman with a briefcase. He wasn't leaning forward and walking fast like he was late to a meeting. Not like he had all the time in the world either. He wasn't on a slow stroll to enjoy the scenery.

His strides were even, each as long as the length of his legs would allow. His shoulders were square and set perpendicular to his path. His gaze was forward, not looking side to side.

He had somewhere to be, I was sure of it, just from watching the way he walked. He wasn't going because someone told him to or because he had to. He was going because he wanted to get there.

GUY WITH NEW SHOES

I look down and see that the guy in front of me is wearing new shoes.

I'm assuming they're new because they're so clean.

Or maybe he's had them for a while and he's just careful about keeping them clean.

If they are new, I wonder if he's proud to be wearing his new shoes out in public.

At some point, they'll get dirty, and he'll no longer think of them as new shoes.

He'll just put them on and leave the house and probably not even remember he's wearing them.

HUMAN ENCYCLOPEDIA

Sitting at a picnic table in the park, sharing a bottle of wine, we spoke. Or rather, he spoke, and I listened.

He talked like an encyclopedia. Every twentieth word was a proper noun. He enunciated the first letter of each word as if to remind me they ought to be capitalized.

At one point, I even thought he might be going in alphabetical order, as he recalled the celebrities he had met while making TV shows and the places he had traveled for filming.

I began to discern the pattern. First, he would say the name. Then, he would pause to see if I had met them or been there, or if I at least knew of the person or had heard of the place. Finally, he would go on to give me the rest of the information, before proceeding to the next person or place.

When I hadn't heard of the person (which was more often than not) and confessed that I hadn't (which I did only a few times, when he looked over the rims of his glasses as if to accuse me of ignorance), he would say, "Oh, they are important, you must read about them." Of a place, he would say, "Oh, it's beautiful, you must go there."

Afterward, walking home, I thought of some possible explanations for his manner of speaking—either he had learned at some point in the past that mentioning names was a way to seem intelligent, or he just wanted to be anyone other than himself, somewhere other than where he was.

TO THE MAN WITH HIS BACK TURNED AT THE RESTAURANT

I do not know you
But I see
You are eating alone
And you seem
To be scholarly
Your side profile
The arm of your glasses
Reaching behind your ear
Your elbows
On the table
The way
You sip your tea
I just know
You are thinking
Masterpieces
Imagining
Wonderlands
Why
Are you alone
When
Was the last time
You shared
Your stories
How can I
Communicate
To you

That I want to hear
What you have to say
About my lauding
Of Nabokov
I would ask you
To pull up a chair
But I'm with my girlfriend
No,
That's not an excuse
I'm shy
Not drunk enough
Not sure if you
Would even want to

EXISTENTIAL
ANXIETY

THE FEEL OF MY FEET ON THE FLOOR

This morning
I can feel my feet
On the floor
More
Than usual
As I walk
To the trash can
To throw away a tissue
It's my heel
Hitting the hardwood
Reverberating
Up through my bones
Beating my eardrums
From the inside
I try
To avoid thinking
About being
In a body
But each step
Reminds me

I LOOK AT MY HANDS

When I wonder how a glass fills with liquid that would otherwise run all over.

Or how things stay in their places when left there and don't float away.

I hold my palms in front of my face and study the creases, like lines on a map of a new world.

Sometimes they just look like hands.

They don't even look like my own hands.

I flex my fingers to make sure they are still under my control.

Curl them to form a fist.

Dig my nails into the skin.

I COME APART

I need something to chew on, to feed me, to metabolize and make work my body that lives and breathes in obedience to the laws of nature that we studied in school—for all those years, until now, when the questions that come rushing in are the ones we were never taught to ask.

With nothing to bite onto, my jaw jabbers until it detaches, my brain liquifies and oozes out of my ears, my limbs separate at the joints.

The parts I previously thought constituted myself disassemble and return to the one homogenous universal element that fills all of space and time and has no name other than the various divine denominations the religions have invented over the years.

TRYING TO KEEP UP A CONVERSATION

As I catch a brief glimpse behind the veil of my routine assumptions, I see that he is living, breathing, and speaking across the table from me.

Just the fact that we can sit here and talk. That we are conscious beings capable of communicating our thoughts. That we are both alive, together, in this moment.

When not taken for granted, this seems truly incredible.

So much that I must resist the urge to stand up from the table, jump up and down, wave my arms, and exclaim, "This is it!"

I would grab my friend by the shoulders, look into his eyes, and ask, "Are you feeling this?"

But I fear that he would not understand.

So I smile politely. Take a sip of my drink. Nod my head.

MY ELUSIVE MAGNUM OPUS

There's only one story I want to write. It's short, dense. Elusive as a fly. Ephemeral as a breeze. And it's not like other stories. I call it a story, but it's not. I only imagine it as one because I'm a writer. Perhaps it can't even be put into words.

I read it just now when I was in the kitchen, making a smoothie. I reached into the jar to scoop protein powder, and there it was. My hand, my fingers, the scoop, the powder—holding space, being.

Being, yes. But how? Because it all actually is? Or just because I can see and feel it? Don't answer that question. There is no answer, just an endless rabbit hole of futile philosophy.

When I reach into the jar, I am suddenly aware that I control my fingers. Around me, there is more. Like my fingers, but not the same. Material, but not me.

The two—my body and the material world—are connected. They communicate, dance. Each can cause the other to change. I pick up the scoop; it raises in the air. I dip the scoop into the powder; it fills.

It is all here! Around me, as I sit at the table, writing. The chairs are pushed in under the table. The candlesticks stand in the center of the table. The light comes in through the window.

I can see it! I can pick up one of the candlesticks, close the blinds. I can change it. Change what I am seeing. Go closer to it, see it in more detail. Smells from a bakery. I can go there. Open the door. Taste the bread.

I wish to convey the marvel of it. I am not concerned with the actual, the facts, the science, the philosophy. Rather, I am more concerned with the experience.

What are the words? For the moment when reality reveals itself. To express appropriate awe in the midst of sheer existence. To worship God for his creation.

IT IS WHAT IT IS

So many books since the printing press, until the final book will say it's not a book that will say it.

Its isness smiles smugly as you try to explain. But how can one explain what it is to be, other than by being?

How can you look at me and say words when we're as in love as we are? Don't you feel it?

Didn't your teachers always bore you? But you learned to stay in your seat. Learned to study and remember.

All while the mountains stood still and the rivers ran. While what was stayed the same and still is.

Because it all just is. And that's it.

We thought we were onto something. We thought we could solve the meaning of life with a math equation, make art as beautiful as nature.

But it was already solved, already beautiful.

Even before us. It already was.

SILENT WHITE ROOM AT NIGHT

Face down
In a room of all white
The sheets are white
The drapes are white
The walls are white
Even the chandelier is white
But the bulbs are clear
And the floor is the color of wood

A creak in the wall
Is the first sound I've heard
Other than a car outside

I could go on and on
Even about nothingness
Probably forever
Combining the same words
In different orders

Even if I wrote it all
And you read it all
You wouldn't remember

It's not the words
There's something behind them
But it's not the dictionary definitions
It's more than that

Or maybe it's less
It's the silent white room at night
It's the singularity of all words

It's the fact that
At any moment
It is what it is
And that's not too complicated

It just is what it is
And the words try to say that
But the more we write
The more we read
The further away we get

It just is
Right here
Right now
And the writing is a dance around it

It's really the sheet against my cheek
The static sound of silence
And there I go again
With the words

It just is
What it is
And that's it
That's all of it

MY THROAT STILL BURNS

I have a hunch that the art we know about isn't the best there ever was. The best probably just came and went without being captured, either because it happened too fast, or it couldn't be translated into one of the common forms we've learned to call "art."

It might have been a tune whistled by a bum lying on his cardboard in the middle of the night when there was nobody there to hear. But maybe even that is too cheap and cliché. An unseen leaf blowing in the wind. Too obvious and trite.

My view is too narrow. Too human. Too here and now. We make art that we understand. Which makes sense, I suppose. I don't know.

Lying here in bed, getting sober, my throat still burns from the cigar. It's 2:45 a.m. A car drives by. I slept all day, then we went over to Jake's for dinner.

After dinner, we went up on the roof and started drinking. We talked and talked, but we didn't really say it. Maybe someone has already said it to me before and I just couldn't quite understand at the time. Even if someone said it to me once, I'd want to hear it again.

In some rare moments, when I can avoid overcomplicating it, I can see straight through to the beating heart of the cosmos.

I saw it in the white ceiling when I woke up from a nap earlier today. I thought to myself, just the fact that I can see that white ceiling, even that is more than I can truly appreciate.

And I don't know why, but that's when I think of dying. I think, I will die and I won't be able to look at a white ceiling like this ever again, and I want to cry.

EVENING-ONSET THANATOPHOBIA

NIGHTS

When sleep seems
Too much like death

I lie awake
Looking at the ceiling

Seeing details
In the darkness

Hearing the hum
Of silence

Longing
For dawn

SLEEP IN THE CITY

I take a bite of the sidewalk and fall back between the cracks. Is it still vipassana then? If my mind is not allowed to wander any further than the sirens and bus stop conversations coming through the open window.

It's too hot, so we have to choose each night—sweat through the sheets, or open the window and let in the noise that even earplugs with a Noise Reduction Rating of 33 can't block out.

We have ice packs in the freezer. I can wrap one of those in an old t-shirt and get my temperature low enough to fall asleep. But by midnight, sometimes earlier, the ice pack has melted, so the window gets opened eventually.

And then we have another choice—put in the earplugs and try not to hear, or meditate on the chaotic city sounds.

I still can't do this successfully. Some primal part of me can't forget that loud noises mean danger and my writer's mind has a hard time hearing conversations without listening to the words being said.

I try not to judge. I try to just listen. But I still miss the pitch-black, silent nights in Montana.

ELEGY

Old men
At the coffee shop
Read today's paper
Reminiscing
About yesterdays
Years ago

My father always said
He felt 20
Even when he was 40
But he's almost 60 now
And it's been a while
Since he's said that

In the morning
It seems like
It'll never end
At night
I'm afraid
To die

The long days
Are an illusion
As the short years
Add up
And I'm a summer month
In between

Young enough
To remember January
Old enough
To fear December
Staring at the sun
In mid-July

I still can't believe
This will ever end
That it has to end
That that's just
The way things are
We're born to die

And all I can do
Is type faster
To get the words down
While I still can
To survive death
In some form

To write an epic
In an afternoon
To live an eternity
In a lifetime
To at least
Have stories to tell

When I'm in a wheelchair
Holding a cup of coffee
Hand shaking
Pinching croissant crumbs
With wrinkly fingers
Watching the snow fall

THE NIGHT COMES FOR ME

Like a lioness stalking her prey.

I am distracted in the daytime.

Even as the sun sets, some light still stands between us.

But I can hear her slow steps in the tall grass at dusk.

I am somehow always surprised when she pounces.

Darkness descends and I am alone again in the belly of the beast.

EGO DEATH

QUARTER-TAB SWIM

I took off my clothes
And walked toward the water

Out to waist-high
A wave came

I dove in
And under

Everything ceased to exist.

Even as the ego dissociates, the body can still remain
lightly with a subdued awareness of the senses.

Under the freezing water, however, that awareness is
obliterated.

There is only the freezing all over. The roar of water
forever. And waves crashing above like the world is
falling apart.

Forgetting to breathe because the art of being
underwater takes precedence for my attention.

My lungs shout, return to the surface! But I cannot hear
them.

The will of nature-at-large overwhelming my individual need to survive.

It making no difference whether my body, a small part of all this, will rise to the surface and swim back to the beach, or drown here and become one with the ocean.

IN THE WOODS IN MONTANA

Large black ants crawl on the Mexican blanket.

Shadows move in tandem with the clouds floating between the sun and the ground.

My friends are talking on the deck above. On the patio below, I sit cross-legged on the blanket, wrists resting on my knees.

Looking out at the trees, I have a desire to put on my shoes and go into the forest.

I am a little off balance now as I walk. And so it begins.

I have found a convenient stump to sit on and write.

All around me, the forest floor is alive. Many ants. Mosquitoes, flying and landing.

As I put my pen to paper, I almost forget the words, but they still come to me somehow, flowing from my surroundings, through my senses, onto the page.

An ant crawls up my leg. Another on my left pointer finger probes with its antennae.

I feel the sun hot on my shoulders through my shirt.

Now I have wandered farther into the woods, where there is some shade.

I wonder how long I have been standing here. My legs have held me, but when I look down at them, I am unsure of how they operate.

Even control of my body seems to be something I could part ways with, if not for the functionality of my fingers holding this pen to write, my legs carrying my sensory organs.

Things occur to me as being beautiful, and in that moment of occurrence, nothing else matters.

My senses are fully immersed in the beauty, like the sight of a crumbling tree trunk, split open and filled with forest debris.

So dead, but so perfectly at home. Sprouts already reaching through the old tree's remains.

A bug lands on my hand. I look to make sure it is not a mosquito. So what if it is?

The wind blows through my hair as it does through the leaves in the trees.

A moment ago, it was dark. The clouds covered the sun. I was scared of what I could not see among the trees. I was alone.

Now the sun shines through and the birds chirp.

I hear my friends laughing in the distance, and I smile.

I am surprised to feel my facial muscles smiling.

I am resistant to going back, to have to talk.

But I know it will be hard to stay out here for too long.

I do not know the ways of the woods. I would starve, get eaten.

I want to survive, and so begins the civilization of man.

In the distance, beyond the trees, I see a runner, trucks on the road. A feeling of familiarity.

I swat away the mosquitoes, brush the ants off my arms, and start back toward the house.

THIS IDEA OF THERE BEING AN OUTSIDE

Through the drapes
The leaves shake

Something
About the separation

Inside
It's hardwood floors

Plaster walls
Soft sheets

Out there
It's wind

Rain
And sky

And there's
Just

Something
About the separation

AT HOME IN THE WORLD

Sidewalk hallways
Skyline ceiling

I've been feeling
At home

Even outside
Of our apartment

I peel away
My wallpaper skin

Unlatch and open
My window eyes

Take off my shoes
In the park

Fall asleep
In the grass

PART OF IT

It all appears
To me now

Getting in
Through my senses

Inside of me
Somehow

Making me feel
As part of it

Pouring in
And back out

LOOKING IN THE MIRROR

In the instant before
I recognize myself
I see

Pimply skin
Lopsided pectorals
Crooked jaw

Rectangular prism
Cylinder
Cube

Color
Light
Dimension

IN BETWEEN DREAMS AND REALITY

My mind swims in the stream of dreams that is ever less related to experiences from my own lifetime. There are added elements from movies, books, and my imagination. Scenes I have only seen or heard about secondhand.

I pass through these scenes, sometimes as myself, other times as someone else. Sometimes I am no one. I am only observing what happens without participating.

When I awake, I am surprised to find myself back within my own body and mind. At first, I feel contained. I feel that my wide-open dream perception has been narrowed into a limited point of view.

I can still close my eyes and imagine, but it is less powerful, tethered to awareness of being in my own body, tied down by the constant reminders from my senses that I am bonded to a singular somatic experience in a certain location at a specific time in a physical world—hearing the traffic noise outside, feeling the bed beneath my back.

BREWING TEA IN A GLASS POT

Beads of moisture born into bulbous bodies
Sag from the underside of the concave lid

In the beginning, each is not yet itself
Indistinguishable in the primordial pot

Then the ocean water evaporates
A chosen few transcend the ethereal layer

On the lid, each bead becomes individual
Thin borders of dryness separate them

They are themselves; alone, but together
In community with others nearby

Aging as gravity weighs on their mortal forms
A gradual descent from apex to edge

On their way, they travel through the dry land
Join with other beads, lose their individuality

Larger beads form, grow heavier
Gain momentum toward the edge

Then drip
Death, rebirth

PURGATORY

My soul, since having ceased to be mine, jockeys for bodily position in the pool of purgatory where all souls queue en masse. Seeking flesh destined for another set of spacetime events similar to the physical life that preceded its most recent death, my soul searches, hoping to live again in individual form.

In the ether of all souls joined together as One, we mingle, and meanwhile, many forget having forgotten their individual lives. It is the same amnesia on either side of the divine line: forgetting what it was like to belong to the One on the earth side, and forgetting what it was like to be an individual on the heaven side.

Until the ethereal ocean lifts out of itself and prepares to precipitate its omnipresence into tiny ignorant droplets, which will once again rain down and fail to remember their former divine lives immediately after being born into another life on earth.

Made in the USA
Monee, IL
21 January 2024

51534997R00060